Valerie Reynolds

A·B·C's
OF
Lunch

illustrated by Terri Osborne
written by Dandi

A is **a**pple
for my lunch.

Some **b**ananas
in a **b**unch.

C for **c**arrot sticks
I'll take.
I love the **c**runchy
sound they
make!

Dd **D**elicious **d**onuts taste so sweet!

Ee **E**ating **e**ggs just can't be beat!

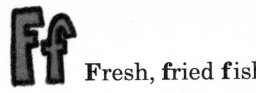

Fresh, fried fish with fishy smell,

Gobs of grapes
should work quite well.

Hh

Hot dogs,
hamburgs,
ham and more!

I i

**Ice cream!
I scream,
"I want
more!"**

J j

Jelly sandwich
meets the test!

Jelly beans on
all the rest.

Kk

Maybe **kiwi**?
Maybe not.

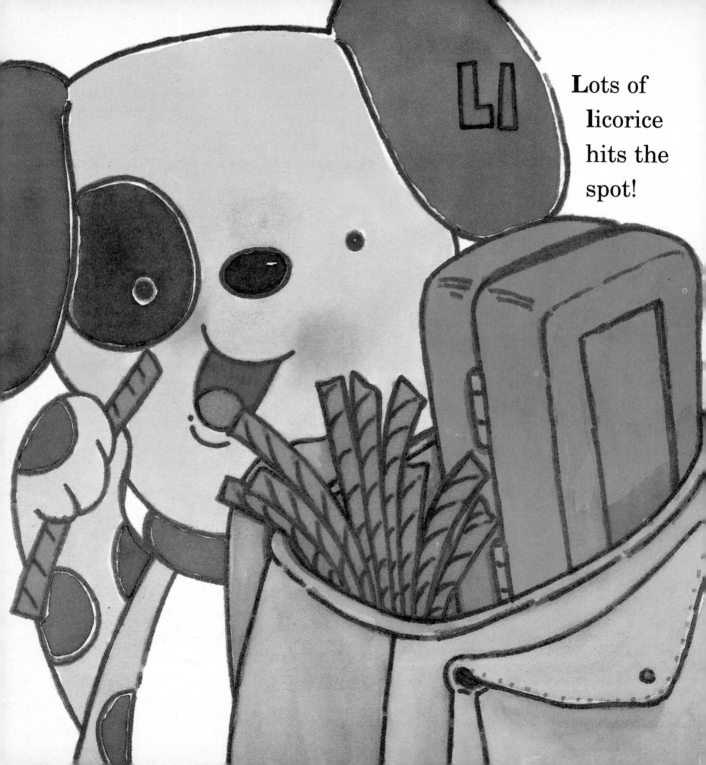

Lots of
licorice
hits the
spot!

Macaroni,
if you
please.
Macaroni,
major
cheese.

Nn

Nuts like walnuts, pecans too.

"Here's some **o**atmeal just for you!"

Peanut butter
for all meals!
Plus, I love
the way it feels!

"**Q**uick, **q**uick!
The bus is here!
Grab your lunch box!
Never fear!"

R r Share your **r**aisins with a friend.

S s **S**ome **s**paghetti has no end!

T is **t**urkey
and
tangerine.

Upside-down
cake,
one green
bean.

V for **v**egetables
and **v**eal,

Very good for
every meal.

Ww

**Watermelon is
for me!
Water –
a necessity.**

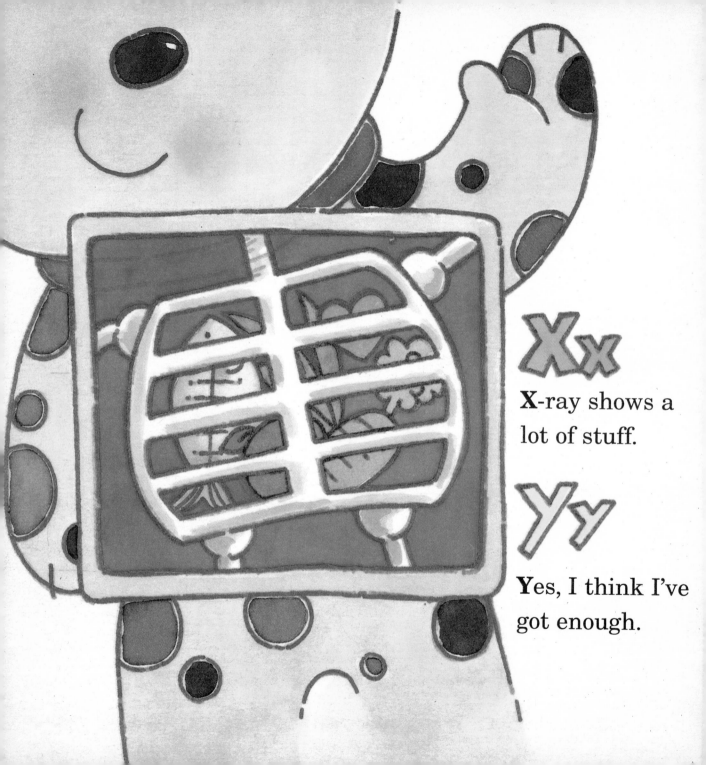

Xx

X-ray shows a lot of stuff.

Yy

Yes, I think I've got enough.

Even when
my lunch is
through,

I'll have
enough
to feed
a **Zoo!**